He is Risen

_____

To My Friend

_____

From

_____

Date

My Sweet Angel Friend

Artwork by
Teresa Kogut

HARVEST HOUSE PUBLISHERS
EUGENE, OREGON

My Sweet Angel Friend

Artwork copyright © by Teresa Kogut, www.teresakogut.com

Published by Harvest House Publishers
Eugene, Oregon 97402
www.harvesthousepublishers.com

ISBN 978-0-7369-5609-3

Design and production by Garborg Design Works, Savage, Minnesota

For more information regarding art prints featured in this book, please contact:

Linda McDonald, Inc.
5200 Park Road, Suite 104
Charlotte, NC 28209
(704) 370-0057

Harvest House Publishers has made every effort to trace the ownership of all poems and quotes. In the event of a question arising from the use of a poem or quote, we regret any error made and will be pleased to make the necessary correction in future editions of this book.

All Scripture quotations are from the New American Standard Bible®, © 1960, 1962, 1963, 1968, 1971, 1972, 1973, 1975, 1977, 1995 by The Lockman Foundation. Used by permission. (www.Lockman.org)

Printed in China

14 15 16 17 18 19 20 /LP/ 10 9 8 7 6 5 4 3 2 1

Love

If instead of a gem, or even a flower, we could cast
the gift of a lovely thought into the heart of a friend,
that would be giving as the angels give.

George MacDonald

Hope is like the wing
of an angel, soaring
up to heaven, and
bearing our prayers to
the throne of God.

Jeremy Taylor

"Stay" is a charming word in a friend's vocabulary.

Louisa May Alcott

Friendship is a strong and habitual

inclination in two persons to promote

the good and happiness of one another.

Eustace Budgell

4

Peace is the first thing the angels sang.

Leo the Great

A friend
loves at
all times.

The Book of Proverbs

I keep my friends as misers do their treasure,
because, of all the things granted us by wisdom,
none is greater or better than friendship.

Pietro Aretino

Walk boldly
and wisely in that
light thou hast—
There is a hand above
will help thee on.

Philip James Bailey

If we would
build on a sure
foundation in
friendship, we must
love friends for
their sake rather
than for our own.

Charlotte Brontë

YOU KNOW ME WELL
AND LOVE ME STILL.

Whatever is to reach the heart must come from above.

Ludwig van Beethoven

YOU ARE MY TREASURED FRIEND.

But all God's angels
come to us disguised.

James Russell Lowell

Little deeds of kindness,
Little words of love,
Make our Earth an Eden,
Like the heaven above.

Julia A. Carney

Every blade
of grass has an
angel bending
over it saying,
"Grow, grow."

Jewish Proverb

8

Life has no blessing
like a prudent friend.

Euripides

Peace

Friendships are fragile things and require as much care in handling as any other fragile and precious thing.

Randolph S. Bourne

Good friends are good for your health.

Sydney Smith

Nothing but heaven itself is better than a friend who is really a friend.

Plautus

Around our pillows golden ladders rise,

And up and down the skies,

With winged sandals shod,

The angels come, and go,

The Messengers of God!

Richard Henry Stoddard, "Hymn to the Beautiful"

I LOVE YOU, MY FRIEND!

Friendship is genuine when two friends can enjoy each other's company without speaking a word to one another.

George Ebers

Friendship is the shadow of the evening, which strengthens with the setting sun of life.

Jean de La Fontaine

12

Hush, my dear, lie
still and slumber,
Holy angels guard
thy bed!
Heavenly blessings
without number
Gently falling on
thy head.

Isaac Watts

Friendship throws
out deep roots in
honest hearts.

Alexander Dumas

FRIENDS TO THE END.

There is nothing like putting the shine on another's face to put the shine on our own.

William Channing Gannett

We see them not—we cannot hear
The music of their wing—
Yet know we that they sojourn near,
The Angels of the spring!

They glide along this lovely ground
When the first violet grows:
Their graceful hands have just unbound
The zone of yonder rose.

Robert Stephen Hawker

MAY GOD BLESS AND KEEP YOU.

Angels descending,
bring from above,
Echoes of mercy,
whispers of love.

Fanny J. Crosby

A kind heart is a fountain
of gladness, making
everything in its vicinity
to freshen into smiles.

Washington Irving

Friends are the
sunshine of life.

John Hay

WE ARE FRIENDS FOREVER.

I will not wish thee riches nor the glow
of greatness, but that wherever thou go
some weary heart shall gladden at thy smile,
or shadowed life know sunshine for a while.
And so thy path shall be a track of light,
like angels' footsteps passing through the night.

Words on a church wall in Upwaltham, England

Trust in my
affection for you.

Anna Jameson

Angels paint
with sound and
sing with color.

Author Unknown

A friend is, as it were,
a second self.
Marcus T. Cicero

The greatest happiness
in life is the conviction
that we are loved,
loved for ourselves,
or rather loved in
spite of ourselves.
Victor Hugo

I am treating you as my friend,
asking you share my present
minuses in the hope I can ask
you to share my future pluses.
Katherine Mansfield

A FRIEND IS
A PRECIOUS
GIFT FROM GOD.

Do not neglect to show hospitality to strangers, for by this some have entertained angels without knowing it.

The Book of Hebrews

The greatest sweetener of human life is friendship.

Joseph Addison

GOOD FRIENDS ARE LIKE ANGELS.

Music is well said to be the speech of angels.

Thomas Carlyle

Be slow in choosing a friend, slower in changing.

Benjamin Franklin

Glory Glory!

The love of heaven
makes one heavenly.

William Shakespeare

SIDE·BY·SIDE &

My friend peers in on me with merry
Wise face, and though the sky stay dim,
The very light of day, the very
Sun's self comes in with him.

A.C. Swinbourne

Silently one by one,
In the infinite meadows of Heaven,
Blossomed the lovely stars,
The forget-me-nots of the Angels.

Henry Wadsworth Longfellow

A pure friendship
inspires, cleanses,
expands, and
strengthens the soul.

Horatio Alger

Agreement in likes and dislikes—
this, and this only, is what
constitutes true friendship.

Lucius Sergius Catilina

HEART·TO·HEART

Love is flower-like;
Friendship is like a
sheltering tree.

Samuel Taylor Coleridge

OUR FRIENDSHIP IS
A SPECIAL GIFT.

Then come the wild weather,
come sleet or come snow,
We will stand by each other,
however it blow.

Simon Dach

Let us not
be justices of
the peace, but
angels of peace.
Saint Theresa of Lisieux

A friend is a present
you give yourself.
Robert Louis Stevenson

GOD IS LOVE

Let me benefit from you in the Lord; refresh my heart in Christ.

The Book of Philemon

But friendship is precious, not only in the shade, but in the sunshine of life; and thanks to a benevolent arrangement of things, the greater part of life is sunshine.

Thomas Jefferson

There is as much greatness of mind in acknowledging a good turn, as in doing it.

Seneca

Love is all very well in its way, but friendship is much higher: Indeed, I know of nothing in the world that is either nobler or rarer than a devoted friendship.

Oscar Wilde

Ah, how good it feels! The hand of an old friend.

Henry Wadsworth Longfellow

Few delights can equal the mere presence of one whom we utterly trust.

George MacDonald

For all we know of what the Blessed do above is, that they sing, and that they love.

Edmund Waller

Many a friendship— long, loyal and self- sacrificing—rested at first upon no thicker a foundation than a kind word.

Frederick W. Faber

Some friendships are as comforting and comfortable as a well-worn pair of shoes. Others are full of excitement and adventure. The best ones are laced with laughter and softened with tears and strengthened with a spiritual bond.

Donna Otto and Emilie Barnes

Greater love
has no one than
this, that one lay
down his life for
his friends.

The Book of John

A beloved friend does
not fill one part of the
soul, but, penetrating
the whole, becomes
connected with all feeling.

William Ellery Channing

Friendship is the
pleasing game of
interchanging praise.

Oliver Wendell Holmes

To each one of us
friendship has a different
meaning. For all of us it is
a gift. Friendship needs
to be cherished and
nurtured. It needs to be
cultivated on a daily basis.
Then shall it germinate
and yield its fruit.

Author Unknown

I believe that if one
always looked at the
sky, one would end
up with wings.

Gustave Flaubert

The simplest
things—a
gentle word,
a soothing
touch—bring
joy and peace
like summer
rain.

Dinah Maria Craik

The guardian angels
of life sometimes fly so
high as to be beyond our
sight, but they are always
looking down upon us.

Jean Paul Richter

You are as welcome
as flowers in May.

Charles Macklin

Blessed are they who
have the gift of making
friends, for it is one of
God's greatest gifts.

Thomas Hughes

YOU ARE MY SWEET ANGEL FRIEND.

There are persons so radiant, so genial, so kind, so pleasure-bearing, that you instinctively feel in their presence that they do you good, whose coming into a room is like the bringing of a lamp there.

Henry Ward Beecher

O continue Your lovingkindness to those who know You.

The Book of Psalms

Sweet souls around us watch us still,
Press nearer to our side;
Into our thoughts, into our prayers,
With gentle helpings glide.

Harriet Beecher Stowe

Love is
a great
beautifier.

Louisa May Alcott

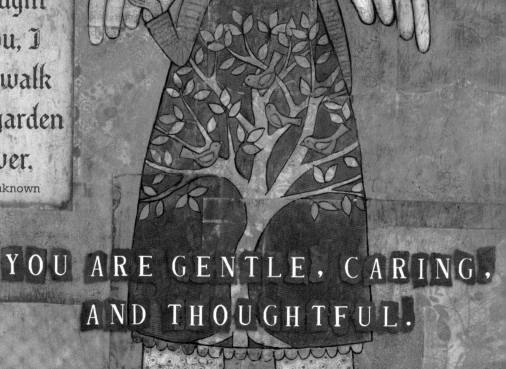

If I planted
a flower
every time
I thought
of you, I
could walk
in my garden
forever.
Author Unknown

YOU ARE GENTLE, CARING,
AND THOUGHTFUL.

He who sows courtesy reaps friendship, and he who plants kindness gathers love.

Saint Basil

Friendship does not spring up and grow great and become perfect all at once, but requires time and the nourishment of thoughts.

Dante

If I have freedom in my love,
And in my soul am free,
Angels alone that soar above,
Enjoy such liberty.

Richard Lovelace

Spring bursts today, for Christ is risen and all the earth's at play. ...sing, creatures, sing, angels and men and birds, and everything...

Christina G. Rossetti

37

All love that has
not friendship for
its base, is like
a mansion built
upon the sand.

Ella Wheeler Wilcox

Gratitude is a nice touch of
beauty added last of all to
the countenance, giving a
classic beauty, an angelic
loveliness, to the character.

Theodore Parker

An angel can
illuminate the thought
and mind of man by
strengthening the
power of vision.

Saint Thomas Aquinas

A friend is a person
with whom I may be
sincere. Before him I
may think aloud.

Ralph Waldo Emerson

THANK YOU FOR BEING MY FRIEND.

The road to a friend's
house is never long.
Danish Proverb

Peaceful

Look round our world; behold the chain of love
Combining all below and all above.

Alexander Pope

So then we pursue the things which make for peace and the building up of one another.

The Book of Romans

You will find as you look back upon your life that the moments when you have really lived are the moments when you have done things in the spirit of love.

Henry Drummond

I have loved you with an everlasting love; therefore I have drawn you with lovingkindness.

The Book of Jeremiah

To love is to believe,
to hope, to know;
'Tis an essay, a taste
of heaven below!

Edmund Waller

Let us be grateful to
people who make us
happy; they are the
charming gardeners who
make our souls blossom.

Marcel Proust

Sleep, my child, and peace attend thee
All through the night.
Guardian angels God will send thee,
All through the night.

Sir Harold Boulton

THE SWEET BLESSINGS OF

The language
of friendship
is not words
but meanings.

Henry David Thoreau

FRIENDSHIP ARE ABUNDANT.

A true friend
is the gift of
God, and he
only who made
hearts can
unite them.

Robert South

Love
is patient.
Love is kind.
♥
1 Corinthians 13:4

The mind never unbends itself so agreeably as in the conversation of a well-chosen friend. There is indeed no blessing of life that is any way comparable to the enjoyment of a discreet and virtuous friend. It eases and unloads the mind, clears and improves the understanding, engenders thought and knowledge, animates virtue and good resolutions, soothes and allays the passions, and finds employment for most of the vacant hours of life.

Joseph Addison

What brings joy to the heart is not so much the friend's gift as the friend's love.

Alfred of Rievaulx

Prayer is the rustling of the wings of the angels who are bringing the blessing to us.

Charles Spurgeon

45

A good laugh makes us better friends with ourselves and everybody around us.

Orison Sweet Marden

YOU ARE SWEET, COMPASSIONATE, AND FAITHFUL.

I have loved my friends as I do virtue, my soul, my God.

Sir Thomas Browne

Yes, we must ever be friends: and of all who offer you friendship let me be ever the first, the truest, the nearest and dearest!

Henry Wadsworth Longfellow

A grateful thought
toward heaven is
of itself a prayer.

Gotthold Ephraim Lessing

Nothing opens the heart
like a true friend, to whom
you may impart griefs, joys,
fears, hopes...and whatever
lies upon the heart.

Francis Bacon